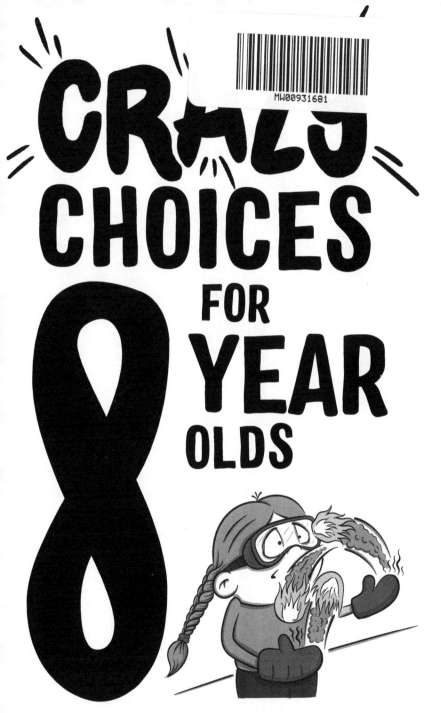

CRAZY CHOICES
FOR
8 YEAR OLDS

A serious talk about (under)pants

Crazy Choices are designed to bamboozle – but some children may be more bamboozled than others. Bathing suit or swimming costume? Washroom or toilet? There's more: sandwiched between the Greek mythology and particle physics you'll also find the occasional poo(p), strategic ~~bogey~~ booger and even a mission-critical ~~bum~~ butt or two. I've mixed and matched to keep everyone happy, I hope – but some choices, words and spelling may lead to a little extra head-scratching!

There's only one thing for it: embrace the bum! Savo~~u~~r the humo~~u~~r, and don't tell your ~~head teacher~~ (or m~~o~~m).

oops **principal**

Design: Fanni Williams / thehappycolourstudio.com
www.matwaugh.co.uk

Produced by Big Red Button Books,
a division of Say So Media Ltd.

ISBN: 978-1-915154-23-1

Published: October 2022
Updated: March 2023

CRAZY CHOICES

MAT WAUGH

ILLUSTRATIONS BY DAVE HALL

How to play
Crazy Choices

A book you can PLAY?
What will they think of next?

 One-player mode

Take book. Read book. Laugh, read bits to your grandpa or cat and say, "Eurgh, that's disgusting!" Test yourself with the Tricky Trivia questions. Finish book. Send winning lottery ticket to me, the author (optional, highly recommended).

 Two-player mode

Grab a friend and a pen and dive into Brainy's Tricky Trivia starting on page 8. For each question, discuss and make your choice: the same or different, you decide!

Each option has a score, depending on whether it's a brainwave or a truly terrible plan. Turn the page to find out who chose the winner and who picked the stinker. Now add your points to the scorecard on page 127. Who's Yoda, and who's useless?

You're all set. Now go crazy!

Mat

MAKE A CRAZY CHOICE!

Trim a lion's claws...

...floss the teeth of a hippo?

Drop a brick on your foot...

OR

...step on a rake?

MAKE A CRAZY CHOICE!

Make friends with any sporting champion **OR** a world-famous musician?

Live in a house without toilet seats **OR** without hot water?

Get trapped in a computer game **OR** on another planet?

BRAINY'S TRICKY TRIVIA!

Hide from lightning in a shed...

OR

see page
10

...in your car?

CRAZY CHOICES FOR 8 YEAR OLDS

Write a story without using the letter 'e'

without vowels?

Have a bad case of astraphobia

or somniphobia?

Be tormented by a terrible toot in the shower

in a small elevator or lift?

SHED vs CAR

If you've been paying attention in science, you might know about **CONDUCTORS**.

Some materials are good conductors of electricity: the current travels through them easily. If your dog has ever chewed through a phone

Totally the wrong type of conductor

(cell) cable, you'll have seen that the wire inside is metal, surrounded by a protective layer of rubber of plastic, and finally a light coating of doggy dribble. Metal is a good conductor and carries the electrical energy to the phone; the rubber or plastic is a bad conductor (called an **INSULATOR**) and stops you getting zapped. The doggy dribble reminds you not to leave phone cables on the floor. So now you know — Whoah! — have you seen that dark sky? A storm is coming. Take shelter! (We're doing science outside).

I can't see a building... Maybe we should make a run for that shed instead? No. That would be a BAD IDEA.

If lightning strikes, there's a good chance the roof might fall on our heads. Ouch.

Maybe we should stay in the car? Cars have rubber tyres. Could that help us? But the car is made of metal — that's a good conductor. We'll be fried like a fritter!

STAY IN THE CAR. Those rubber

Totally the wrong type of car

tyres won't save us: lightning is hotter than the sun! Weirdly, it's the metal that should keep us safe: it acts like a **cage.** The electricity should travel around us and safely down into the ground.

Shed (-5pts) **Car** 5pts

Car beats shed – just don't touch the metal doors!

E vs VOWELS

Surely it's impossible to write a book without the most common letter in the alphabet? (It's in that last sentence 7 times!) Nope — Ernest Wright did it. He wrote a book called Gadsby, which was 50,000 words long and didn't include any Es. Well... almost. When he first published it nearly 100 years ago he included four Es by mistake, but I think we can let him off. It's extremely hard: you try it!

A story without any vowels though... could you read it? I bet you can't!

"nc pn tm thr ws lnly 8-yr-ld wh smlld f cbbg. vn hr frnds clld hr 'vgtble grl' — bt thy ddn't knw bt hr spr pwr..."

E **3pts** Vowels **5pts**

Writing without vowels is hard – reading it is harder!

ASTRAPHOBIA vs SOMNIPHOBIA

Everyone is afraid of something. It might be **SNAKES**, or horses, or heights. And if you're terrified — you shudder and shake, even if you see a picture or think about it — then that's called a phobia. Arachnophobia is the fear of spiders, for instance. But some phobias are more unusual.

ASTRAPHOBIA is no fun: it's the fear of thunder and lightning (even if you're not hiding in the shed!).

Like most parents, I love bedtime. Aaah, lovely sleep! Children aren't so keen. But if it's more than that — if you're terrified of sleep — then you have **SOMNIPHOBIA.**

Astraphobia (-3 pts)   Somniphobia (-6 pts)

A fear of sleep sounds even less fun than a fear of storms. Being afraid is normal, but it can be a horrible feeling. If that's you, ask a grown-up for help.

SHOWER vs ELEVATOR

Let's get one thing clear: it's **YOUR** toot that's causing the stink. But where would be the worst place to **get a nose-full?**

If you were in the shower, would the water wash away the nasty niff? Would the pong float out of the top?

In a lift, could you blame it on somebody else?

> **"ERR, YES, IT WAS A MAN WHO GOT OUT ON THE THIRD FLOOR. I THINK HIS NAME WAS MAT?"**

Don't even try it: I CAN HEAR EVERY WORD.

There's one clear loser here: it's you, in the shower. It smells worse, for longer, because your nose works better when it's warm and damp. Take the lift.

Shower (-7 pts) **Elevator** (-2 pts)

If you chose the shower because you like the smell, deduct an extra five points. Weirdo.

MAKE A CRAZY CHOICE!

Scrap with a swan...

...duel with a duck?

MAKE A CRAZY CHOICE!

Replace your teeth with diamonds **OR** rubies?

Burp to refill your glass **OR** cough to make your teacher do a little boogie?

Flip a coin to decide if you'll be rich all your life **OR** to decide if you'll be healthy?

MAKE A CRAZY CHOICE!

Be an angel...

OR

...a devil?

Sleepwalk...

...talk in your sleep?

MAKE A CRAZY CHOICE!

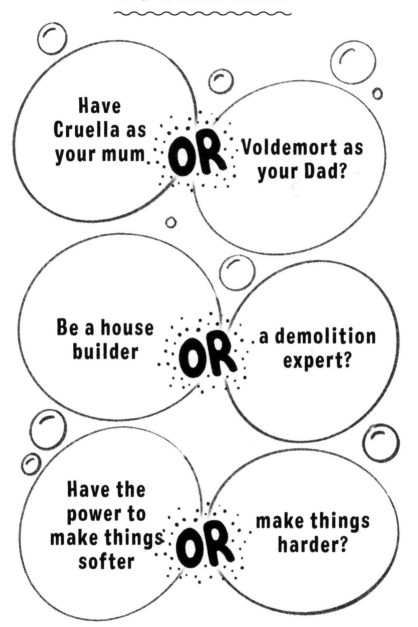

Have Cruella as your mum **OR** Voldemort as your Dad?

Be a house builder **OR** a demolition expert?

Have the power to make things softer **OR** make things harder?

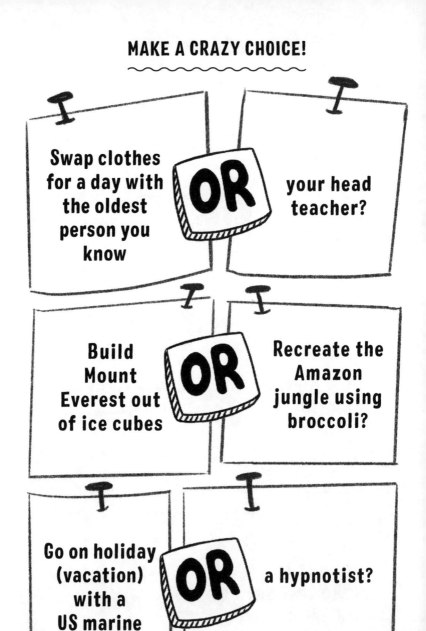

Swap clothes for a day with the oldest person you know **OR** your head teacher?

Build Mount Everest out of ice cubes **OR** Recreate the Amazon jungle using broccoli?

Go on holiday (vacation) with a US marine **OR** a hypnotist?

MAKE A CRAZY CHOICE!

Live on the moon for a year...

OR

...live on the International Space Station?

Lock yourself in
a public toilet
by mistake...

...get stuck
up a
ladder?

OR

Have a million pounds or dollars to spend on eggs **OR** on feathers?

Cook all your own food **OR** do all your own laundry?

Have a nose that picks itself **OR** a bottom that wipes itself?

MAKE A CRAZY CHOICE!

Have a TV on your ceiling that you can watch in bed  a fridge of never-ending snacks in your wardrobe?

Train as a comedian but get a job as a prison officer  train as a prison officer but get a job as a comedian?

Travel to anywhere in the world  travel back in time in your home town?

MAKE A CRAZY CHOICE!

Be stung by a jellyfish...

OR

...bitten by a horse?

BRAINY'S TRICKY TRIVIA!

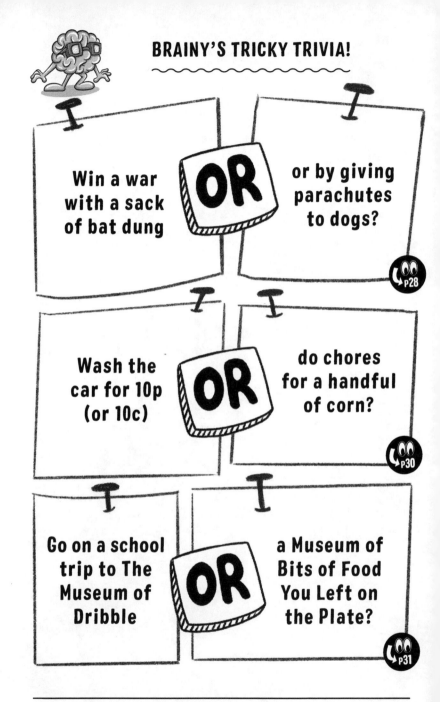

Win a war with a sack of bat dung **OR** or by giving parachutes to dogs?

P28

Wash the car for 10p (or 10c) **OR** do chores for a handful of corn?

P30

Go on a school trip to The Museum of Dribble **OR** a Museum of Bits of Food You Left on the Plate?

P31

BRAINY'S TRICKY TRIVIA!

Buy toilet roll for a panda...

see page 32

OR

...a sloth?

BAT vs DOG

First, take **bat dung** (please do, it stinks). The poo of bats and birds is called guano. It sounds less pooey. You wouldn't be sniffy either if you knew that it used to be worth millions. It was shipped all over the world to be used as fertilizer, and guano also contains a chemical called SALTPETRE. That's an ingredient in gunpowder, and it was used in the American Civil War and World War I. Three cheers for bat poop!

That wasn't the end for bats, though: in World War II, a dentist made a plan to attach tiny firebombs with timers to bats. He called them **bat bombs**. The bats would then be set free over Japan to roost in homes that were mostly made of wood. At a chosen time, cities would go up in flames (and the bats, too ☹).

So far so **nutty**. But then a bunch of bats were released by accident during testing. They found a lovely home right under a fuel tank... and set the whole air force base on fire. Oops. **THE BAT PLAN WAS CANCELLED.**

What about **dogs in parachutes** — is that a barking idea? Nope! We're in World War II again, and troops are being dropped behind enemy lines in France. And to sniff out the explosives, they were joined by dogs in doggy-sized parachutes. Some of them weren't very keen to jump at first, but a meaty treat soon got them leaping!

Bat 7pts **Dog** 10pts

Dogs will do anything for a snack!

PENNIES vs CORN

Pennies or corn for chores?! You should go on strike. Refuse to tidy your room; stop cleaning...

Hang on, there's someone on the phone.

"HELLO? REALLY? NEVER? SURE, I'LL TELL THEM. BYEE!"

So I've just been told that you don't do any of these things anyway — so if you go on strike, who'll notice?

It's a trick question. It doesn't matter which you choose, because who likes corn? Chickens. It's chicken feed. And whether you're 'paid chicken feed' or paid 10p or 10c, it means you're paid something worth very little. (And if you're 'paid peanuts'? Same thing, but for monkeys!)

PENNIES (-5 pts) CORN (-5 pts)

This is an example of an idiom: *words with one meaning that we now use to mean something else.*

DRIBBLE vs LEFTOVERS

 What would a **MUSEUM OF DRIBBLE** look like — little buckets of spit you could peer into? A fountain with saliva spouts? Yuck. You're crazy!

If you chose a **MUSEUM OF LEFTOVERS,** you're also mad (or hungry). But you get a couple of points because there **WAS** a museum like that, in an English cafe. It displayed the bits that famous people hadn't eaten. They included a piece of **TOASTIE** left by a pop star, cake crumbs from a TV presenter and their star attraction — pudding left by **KING CHARLES III,** back when he was plain old Prince Charles. You'll be shocked to know that the tiny museum is now closed.

DRIBBLE (-2 pts) **LEFTOVERS** **2 pts**

One is imaginary, the other is shut.

PANDA vs SLOTH

For MR PANDA, you'll need to stack those toilet rolls high. All that bamboo they eat travels through their digestive system pretty fast. The result? Pandas poo around **40 times** a day. And they poop in their sleep, too.

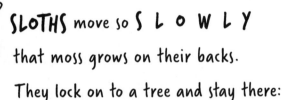

SLOTHS move so S L O W L Y that moss grows on their backs.

They lock on to a tree and stay there: even a jaguar can't pull them off. Sometimes they even hang on after they die. They're colour-blind, can hardly see in dim light, and can't see at all in bright light. It takes them a month to digest a leaf. So you won't need many trips to the supermarket: MR SLOTH HAS A POO ABOUT ONCE A WEEK.

Panda 1pt **Sloth** 6pts

Yucky pandas! Sloths win this one. Very, very slowly.

MAKE A CRAZY CHOICE!

Dream about losing your teeth...

...dream about losing your clothes?

MAKE A CRAZY CHOICE!

Win 10 extra birthday presents by doing 'the plank' for 90 seconds **OR** by answering 20 maths questions in 30 seconds?

Be a grown-up **OR** a child?

Get lost in a forest **OR** in the mountains?

MAKE A CRAZY CHOICE!

Live in a house designed like a huge banana...

OR

...an enormous pair of underpants?

Sneeze for a week...

...or have hiccups for a day?

MAKE A CRAZY CHOICE!

Be the President of the USA  **the Prime Minister of the Bahamas?**

The Bahamas has more than 3,000 beautiful islands!

Wear bacon perfume for a day  **or smell of toffee instead?**

Race against your head teacher (principal)  **your best friend?**

Winner gets a free trip to Disneyland!

MAKE A CRAZY CHOICE!

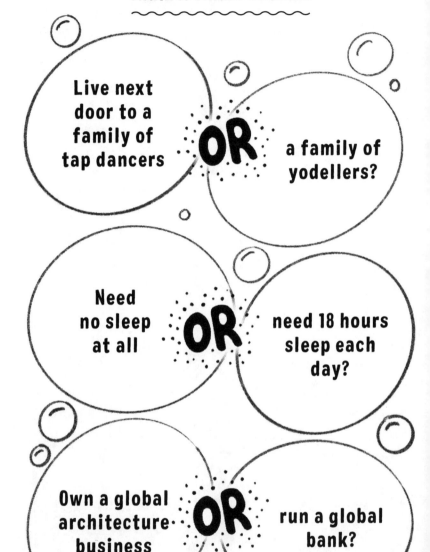

Live next door to a family of tap dancers **OR** a family of yodellers?

Need no sleep at all **OR** need 18 hours sleep each day?

Own a global architecture business **OR** run a global bank?

MAKE A CRAZY CHOICE!

Pedal the length of Africa on a unicycle...

OR

...row the Atlantic
in a bath tub?

BRAINY'S TRICKY TRIVIA!

Jump like an elephant...

OR

...throw like a chimpanzee?

see page 42

CRAZY CHOICES FOR 8 YEAR OLDS

BRAINY'S TRICKY TRIVIA!

Sleep in a prison **OR** a hotel?

p43

Be whacked by a giraffe **OR** kicked by a secretary bird?

p44

Count all the ants in Antarctica **OR** the germs in Germany?

p46

ELEPHANT vs CHIMP

Do you know how much an elephant weighs? Enough to break the springs on your trampoline, that's how much. That's not the only reason they absolutely cannot jump — all the bones in their legs point downwards, like a ballet dancer 'en pointe'. The bones in your feet are **FLAT**, which means you can spring up.

Here's an elephant doing ballet [note to me: check this pic later]

Chimps can definitely throw: they'll chuck rocks, stones and even poo — bleurgh! But chimps and other animals aren't actually very good at it: their shoulders don't work like ours. And that's why you never see a **CHIMP PLAYING DARTS**.

Elephant (0 pts) **Chimp** 3 pts

One Swedish chimp was caught hiding rocks before the zoo opened, to throw at visitors later. Naughty!

PRISON vs HOTEL

In 2017, Saudi Arabia arrested dozens of people, including 11 princes. They were accused of stealing money and taken to a luxury hotel with a swimming pool, bowling alley and spa. Arrest me now! Except these prisoners were told that the only way they could ever leave this luxurious prison was to pay back the money they were accused of stealing. **PETRIFIED, THEY SOON PAID UP.**

But if a hotel-turned-into-a-prison sounds scary, why not try a **PRISON-TURNED-INTO-A-HOTEL** instead? They also have swimming pools and other luxuries. And best of all, you can leave any time you like.

Prison (-3pts) Hotel (-3pts)

I've forgotten which is which, so everybody loses. Complain and I'll add three years to your sentence.

GIRAFFE vs BIRD

Neither of these are good options. Here's why.

Let's start with the giraffe. If you're a human — just checking — then you're very

Gross alert!

unlikely to be attacked by a giraffe. They prefer munching the juicy leaves from the top of acacia trees, and are more likely to lumber away if they get scared.

But those muscly necks don't just give giraffes a good view: males use them **TO FIGHT**. And then when it's time to make giraffe babies, the male giraffe will poke or whack the female giraffe with his neck until she does **A WEE**. And then he drinks it.

You read that right. After a little taste, he can work out whether Mrs Giraffe is ready to have a baby. And you thought giraffes were cute!

Now let me introduce you to the secretary bird, also found in Africa. They're your height and walk on long skinny legs, just like you. They get their name from fancy feathers that look like the end of a quill (an old-fashioned pen made from a feather, used by secretaries). They sound lovely, don't they?

STAY BACK!

They kick their prey to death. Snakes and lizards get stomped and then these frilly killers rip their victims apart with their bills. Or just swallow them whole. **GULP.**

Typical secretary bird shoes [note to me: pic looks weird. Check later.]

Giraffe (-5 pts) **Bird** (-8 pts)

Those vicious secretary birds can't even type!

ANTS vs GERMS

Counting the ants in Antarctica shouldn't take you long: **there aren't any.** It's too chilly for them. There is one critter that lives there: the Antarctic midge. These bugs spend nine months *frozen solid*. Scientists find them in **PENGUIN POO**. Would you like to count them instead? Why are you running away?

Head to Germany to count germs, then. **THEY'RE EVERYWHERE**. Germ is another word for types of bacteria. These are **MICRO-ORGANISMS:** tiny beings you can only see through a microscope. They're part of life. If I took all the bacteria out of you, I could fill a cereal bowl... but *IT WOULD ALSO KILL YOU.* Oops.

Ants `4pts` **Germs** `-3pts`

Counting to zero won't take long,
then it's time to play with the penguins!

MAKE A CRAZY CHOICE!

Find a wasp's nest under your bed...

OR

...hear a rattlesnake outside your bedroom window?

MAKE A CRAZY CHOICE!

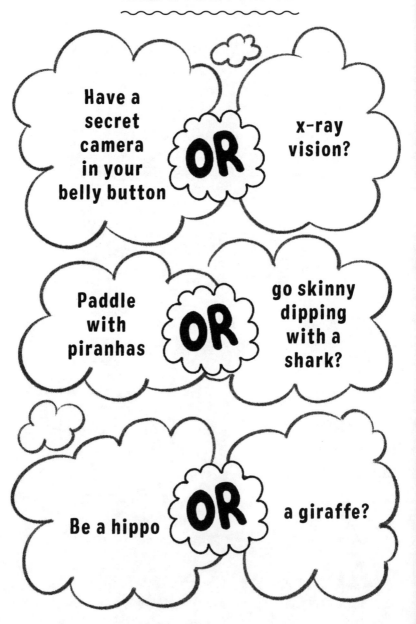

Have a secret camera in your belly button **OR** x-ray vision?

Paddle with piranhas **OR** go skinny dipping with a shark?

Be a hippo **OR** a giraffe?

CRAZY CHOICES FOR 8 YEAR OLDS

MAKE A CRAZY CHOICE!

Do fifty push-ups...

OR

...do a spelling test?

Be able to put your fist in your mouth...

OR

...put your foot in your mouth?

Some bendy people with small hands and big mouths can do both. There's only one way to find out if you're among them!

MAKE A CRAZY CHOICE!

Live to 40 years old and then start getting younger  live to 20 years old and then stay that age?

Get splinters in your foot  have a tummy ache?

Keep money that you find (but you can't tell anyone)  hand the money in (and hope for a reward)?

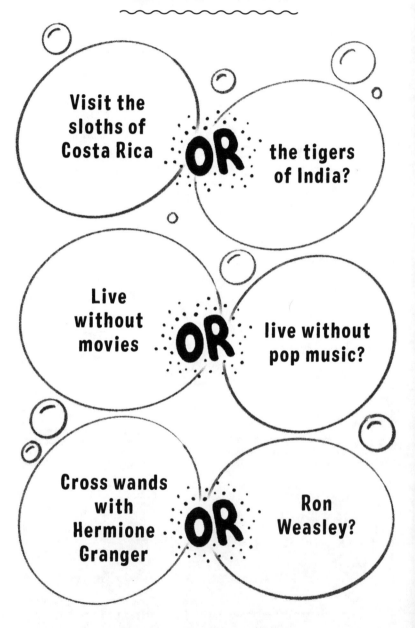

Visit the sloths of Costa Rica **OR** the tigers of India?

Live without movies **OR** live without pop music?

Cross wands with Hermione Granger **OR** Ron Weasley?

MAKE A CRAZY CHOICE!

Grow hair down to your ankles...

OR

...a beard down to your belly button?

BRAINY'S TRICKY TRIVIA!

Build sandcastles on a beach in Spain  **drive at 200mph on a German highway?**

P56

Rub salt into a scrape on your leg  **use sugar instead?**

P57

Saw logs  **sing for your supper?**

P58

BRAINY'S TRICKY TRIVIA!

Go on a roller coaster...

OR

see page 59

...eat a packet of Flamin' Hot Cheetos?

BEACH vs HIGHWAY

Got a bucket and spade? **Watch out!**

Because on some Spanish beaches, building

sandcastles is illegal. (It's also against the law to

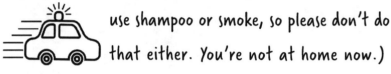 use shampoo or smoke, so please don't do

that either. You're not at home now.)

It's huge sand sculptures that they really don't like,

so you should be OK. But I'm not a lawyer and if

you get arrested, I'll say I've never heard of you.

What about driving at 200mph — that's crazy

and illegal, right? Not in Germany.

On some highways you can drive as

fast as your car can go. But as parents

love to say, **'JUST BECAUSE YOU CAN DO SOMETHING,**

DOESN'T MEAN YOU SHOULD!'

Beach `5pts` **Highway** `2pts`

You can't drive and eat ice cream. Beach wins.

SALT vs SUGAR

If someone **RUBS SALT IN THE WOUND** it means they're making something worse. If you fall over – **ouch!** – and your football coach tells you that you are a terrible player, that's rubbing salt in the wound. The words sting, just like salt would.

Except... that's what sailors used to do. Salt works as an *antiseptic,* helping wounds to heal. But what if there was a **✦magical✦** white powder that works without the hurty bit? There is: **SUGAR!** Apparently it soaks up the moisture which means bacteria can't grow. But doctors prefer bandages and antiseptic ointments. You know what I'm going to say: **DON'T TRY THIS AT HOME!**

Salt `1pt` **Sugar** `1pt`

Don't Try This At Home. Did I mention that?

LOGS vs SINGING

If you say that grandpa is **SAWING LOGS**, you'll maybe find him on the

Idiom alert!

sofa with dribble running down his cheek. He's snoring so loud it sounds like someone sawing logs!

KNOCK KNOCK! Hang on, there's someone at the door. Let's see who it is.

Ah, it's a wandering minstrel! I haven't seen one of these travelling entertainers for 400 YEARS. If she's good, we might give her supper!

🕐 **FIVE MINUTES LATER...**

No, she was dreadful. I told her to go next door. (Someone who **SINGS FOR THEIR SUPPER** is anyone who does some work in return for something they need.)

Logs 4pts Singing 2pts
Lovely, glorious sleep beats work any day!

COASTER vs CHEETOS

When you eat **spicy foods,** it really does feel like your mouth is burning. The food has **TRICKED** you, but the feeling is the same! Children who eat spicy food when they're small eat more when they're grown up. But why do some people like it, and others not?

Some scientists think that it is because spice lovers have learned to get a thrill from the chilli heat, a bit like the thrill you get from a **ROLLER COASTER.** So if you like roller coasters, then you probably like gobbling up **CHILLI SNACKS.** And if you hate theme parks, you may also prefer a bowl of **creamy pasta** instead!

Coaster `4 pts` **Cheetos** `4 pts`

It's a dead heat, say the men in white coats.

MAKE A CRAZY CHOICE!

Have an extra leg...

OR

...an extra arm?

MAKE A CRAZY CHOICE!

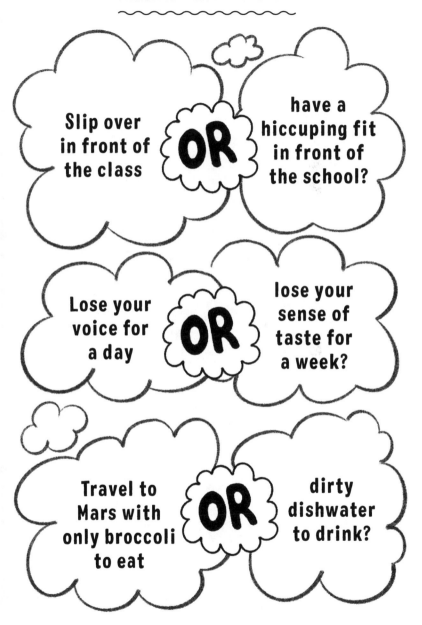

Slip over in front of the class **OR** have a hiccuping fit in front of the school?

Lose your voice for a day **OR** lose your sense of taste for a week?

Travel to Mars with only broccoli to eat **OR** dirty dishwater to drink?

MAKE A CRAZY CHOICE!

Have a garden with no flowers  **OR** a garden without grass?

Practise your times tables on your birthday  **OR** do spelling tests on Christmas Day?

Find Willy Wonka's Golden Ticket  **OR** have your own Great Glass Elevator?

MAKE A CRAZY CHOICE!

Grow horns like a rhino...

...fur like a monkey?

MAKE A CRAZY CHOICE!

Shoot lightning bolts from your fingers...

...clap as loud as thunder?

MAKE A CRAZY CHOICE!

Belly-flop in the Olympic diving finals **OR** trip over in the 100m sprint?

Discover a way to live without drinking **OR** find a way to live without eating?

Have a busy day **OR** a lazy day?

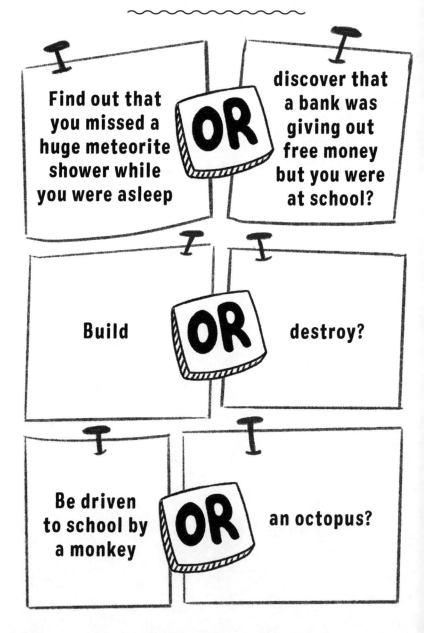

Find out that you missed a huge meteorite shower while you were asleep **OR** discover that a bank was giving out free money but you were at school?

Build **OR** destroy?

Be driven to school by a monkey **OR** an octopus?

MAKE A CRAZY CHOICE!

Eat spaghetti a mile long...

...drink a bucket of fizzy drink?

Go over the world's highest waterfall in a barrel...

OR

...in a submarine?

see page 70

Go on another school trip: this time it's to The Ironing Board museum **OR** head instead to the Dog Collar Museum?

P72

Get sweaty feet **OR** get sweaty ears?

P73

Eat baby food for koalas **OR** baby food made to a 100-year-old recipe?

P74

BARREL vs SUBMARINE

Going over waterfalls in a barrel is a $silly$ thing to do. But as you know, grown-ups can be extremely silly. So lots of them have tried it at **NIAGARA FALLS,** perhaps the most famous waterfall in the world. Many drowned. Some survived, but were arrested (because it's illegal).

But smartypants readers will know that the highest waterfall is **ANGEL FALLS** in Venezuela, around 20 times higher. What a whopper. Let's go!

Sorry — the Royal Danish Navy is on the phone. They always call when I'm busy.

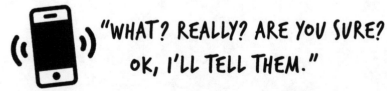

"WHAT? REALLY? ARE YOU SURE? OK, I'LL TELL THEM."

Hi! I'm back. Change of plan: the Danes have found something. You'll need a submarine. Got one?

Great! Then head for the Denmark Strait, the water that separates Iceland and Greenland. There you'll discover an underwater waterfall or cataract: at 3.5km (around 2 miles) high, that's **70** Niagaras!

HOW DO YOU PILOT A SUB OVER A WATERFALL? How should I know? You'll work it out, I'm sure.

HOW CAN A WATERFALL BE UNDERWATER? Hang on, I'll Google it. Do I have to do *everything?*

Ah, yes. Cold water from one sea meets warmer water from another. The cold water sinks, because that's what cold water does — try adding some to your bath — and tumbles over an underwater cliff. Simple. Now off you pop!

Barrel (−8 pts) **Submarine** **3 pts**

Only bozos take the barrel. Submarines for the win!

BOARD vs COLLAR

Do you still want to go on a school trip after that awful visit to the Leftovers Museum (page 31)? You must be desperate to get out of your maths lesson if you want to visit an **IRONING BOARD MUSEUM.** And

Ironing? Bored.

you're out of luck, because it doesn't exist. So you and your WRINKLY PANTS will have to find another museum to visit.

And I know just the place. The Dog Collar Museum, inside Leeds Castle, England. Hundreds of them: **FANCY** collars, **PLASTIC** collars, **LEATHER** collars, **ENGRAVED** collars. (There's just one mystery: why isn't it called Leads Castle?)

Ironing Board (0 pts) **Collar** (1 pt)

Maybe a maths lesson really isn't that bad?

FEET vs EARS

Sweat is produced by glands that are all over your body, but particularly in your feet. Adult feet produce enough sweat to fill a glass, every day. Imagine drinking your parent's foot sweat. Eurrrrgh.

Do you know what else is sweat? Earwax. It's sweat mixed with dead skin cells, waxes and oils. Yummy.

Here's another thing. Is your earwax wet (orange and waxy), or dry (flaky and grey or white)? The world is split into those who get wet or dry wax.

BONUS FACT: if you have dry earwax, your feet and armpits don't get very whiffy!

Feet ⟨ -2 pts ⟩ **Ears** ⟨ -4 pts ⟩

If your earwax is dry, swap the scores.
If you thought this was gross, wait for page 88...

Koalas are a furry bundle of cute, aren't they? They're not bears, whatever people say, but marsupials, like kangaroos. That means they carry their babies, called joeys, around in a pouch for six months (HOW CUTE!). And then the babies ride on their mums' backs for another six months (HOW CUTE!). They can sleep for up to 18 hours a day (HOW CUTE!). And mums feed their babies their own poop (HOW CU— hey say WHAT?)

You heard me. Baby koalas can't digest eucalyptus leaves when they're small, so their mum eats them and feeds THE BROWN STUFF to her joey, along with a little milk to wash it down. Koala experts call it **pap** rather than poo, but you can call it anything you want: **I'M FULL, THANKS.**

So let's buy some of this **NEW BABY FOOD** that went on sale around a hundred years ago. This range of new soups was made in many flavours including vegetable, pea, spinach and...

liver. Animal livers, full of vitamins, whizzed up and put in a can. Yum. No, **YOU** have first helpings, I insist.

Thirsty? Try some refreshing milk — straight from **THE GOAT**. In Ancient Greece (and even when your grandparents were small), goats were sometimes used when mums weren't around. Babies were plopped under the goat, shown where to suck, and slurped away!

Koala pap (-5 pts) **Baby food** (-3 pts)

Pap makes liver soup look delicious. Incredible.

MAKE A CRAZY CHOICE!

Play basketball with a tennis ball...

OR

...tennis with a basketball?

MAKE A CRAZY CHOICE!

Be taught by Cyborg  Beast Boy?

Go to a fancy dress party as Mr Angry  a ball of belly button fluff?

Have an extra birthday each year  go on an extra holiday?

MAKE A CRAZY CHOICE!

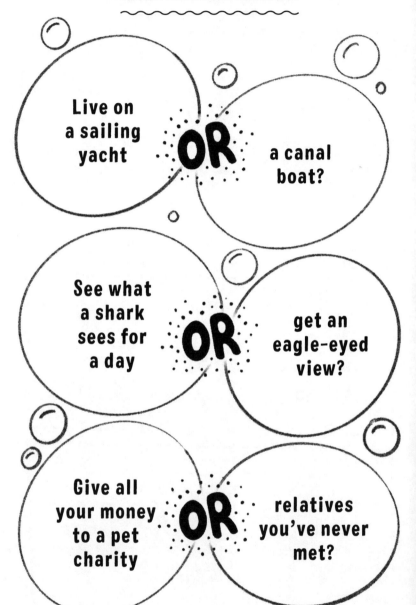

Live on a sailing yacht **OR** a canal boat?

See what a shark sees for a day **OR** get an eagle-eyed view?

Give all your money to a pet charity **OR** relatives you've never met?

Smash a coconut with a jellyfish...

OR

...dance a tango with a rhino?

Wear a t-shirt made of lasagne...

OR

...underpants made of bread?

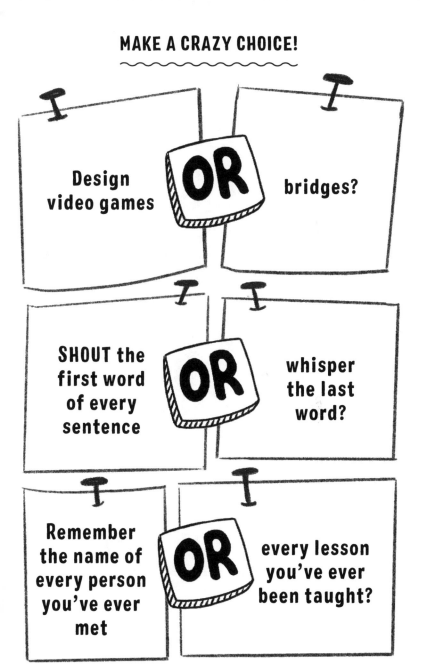

Design video games **OR** bridges?

SHOUT the first word of every sentence **OR** whisper the last word?

Remember the name of every person you've ever met **OR** every lesson you've ever been taught?

Live without your adenoid **OR** your little toes?

p84

Blame that funny smell on the dog **OR** termites?

p86

Stay as cool as a cucumber **OR** cool as a cabbage?

p87

Save
all your
earwax...

OR

...save all your hair clippings?

see page
88

Your **adenoid** is a shy little lump hidden high up inside your nose to catch infections. Sometimes, it swells up and if you're still young, it might be removed in a teensy operation.

Your adenoid is hiding up here

And as soon as your adenoid is removed, **you drop down dead.**

Hang on, there's a doctor on the phone. Back in a sec.

"WHAT'S THAT? NO, I STUDIED POETRY. WHY DO YOU ASK? ARE YOU SURE? AH. RIGHT. I'LL TELL THEM."

So I'm back. It turns out I made a ᴛɪɴʏ mistake. Where I wrote 'YOU DROP DOWN DEAD', I should have written 'YOU EAT ICE CREAM, FEEL BETTER AND FORGET ABOUT IT, BECAUSE YOU REALLY DON'T NEED YOUR ADENOID.' Doctors are so fussy about facts!

Talking of little things, we don't need those **LITTLE TOES**, do we? They just rub on new shoes. Let's ask if the hospital can **chop them off** at the same time.

Hang on, it's that doc on the phone AGAIN. Pfft.

"WHAT IS IT NOW? NO, I DON'T HANG FROM TREES. WHAT A SILLY QUESTION. CAN'T YOU SEE I'M BUSY?"

I was right! Pinky toes are pretty much useless. You can walk, run and even hop without them, though hanging from a tree like a sloth would be tricky. Humans might even **EVOLVE WITHOUT THEM** one day (little toes, not sloths).

Adenoid `4 pts` **Toes** `2 pts`

You'd look weird without little toes. Adenoid wins!

DOG vs TERMITE

When it comes to **BOTTOM BURPS,** dogs are shameless. And they pong. So when your parent *floats a stinker* they point at Luna and pretend it was her.

But maybe **HE WHO DENIED IT, SUPPLIED IT?** on average we all trump 15 times, day and night.

The most farty animal in the world isn't actually a dog, or your mum or dad. It's the **TERMITE.** But you can't smell termite toots, so don't blame them.

Why don't we say it was a honey badger? They let out a smell so awful it stuns bees. The badgers then sneak into the hive and steal the honey!

Bees should use these on their noses

Dog `5 pts` Termite `0 pts`

(Lose 10 points if that awful stench was you!)

CUCUMBER vs CABBAGE

CUCUMBERS are cool. I don't mean that they look good in sunglasses; I mean that cucumbers are your friend on a hot day. You could make cold cucumber soup (delicious, I promise); rub it on your sunburn, or put slices over your eyes (looks weird, feels nice).

But **CABBAGE** has its admirers, too, even if you're not one of them. Babe Ruth, one of the most famous baseball players of all time, ate a lot of hotdogs and drank a lot of beer. But he was also a cabbage fan. To keep cool, he'd grab a couple of chilled cabbage leaves and put them under his cap.

Cucumber 7pts Cabbage 9pts

Any 8-year-old that chooses cabbage is my hero.

EARWAX vs HAIR

If you have a cat or a dog, there's only one word they want to hear you say: **earwax.** Animals love the **SMELL** and the **TASTE** — especially the orange version. But keep it in your ear, not the cat, because earwax traps dirt and bacteria and may even act as an insect repellant.

Good news: earwax candles don't exist

Hair clippings normally go straight in the bin or the compost heap. But some hairdressers in France send their clippings off to be squeezed into tubes and used to **TRAP OIL** spilled at sea. It's highly absorbent and can be cleaned to be used over and over again!

Earwax (0 pts) **Hair** (5 pts)

Get a French haircut, save the planet!

MAKE A CRAZY CHOICE!

Do a forward roll every time a door slams  do a cartwheel whenever you hear a car horn?

Spend a week eating upside down  holding your cutlery with your feet?

Be a polar explorer  a deep sea adventurer?

Be funny...

OR

...be serious?

MAKE A CRAZY CHOICE!

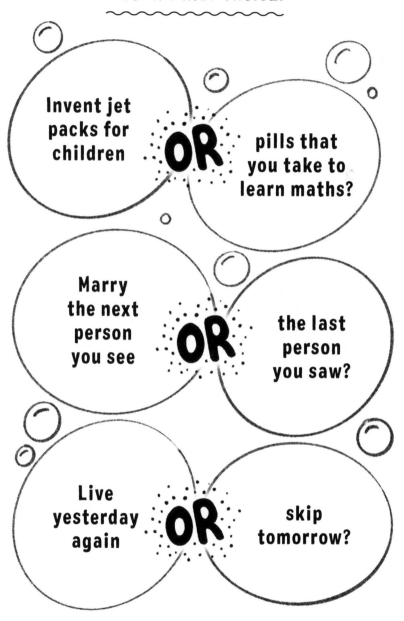

Invent jet packs for children **OR** pills that you take to learn maths?

Marry the next person you see **OR** the last person you saw?

Live yesterday again **OR** skip tomorrow?

MAKE A CRAZY CHOICE!

Live without sugar **OR** live without any red food?

Be rich but unable to remember anything **OR** poor with an excellent memory?

Learn a poem every day **OR** learn a few words of a foreign language?

MAKE A CRAZY CHOICE!

Have candles for fingers...

OR

...Cheetos or Wotsits for toes?

MAKE A CRAZY CHOICE!

Be the best singer in class...

...the best dancer?

MAKE A CRAZY CHOICE!

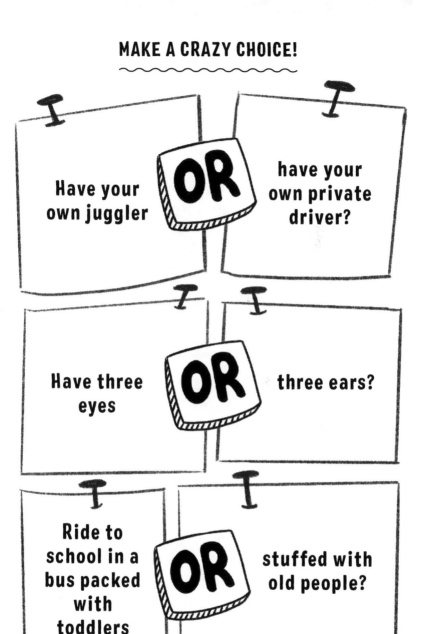

Have your own juggler **OR** have your own private driver?

Have three eyes **OR** three ears?

Ride to school in a bus packed with toddlers **OR** stuffed with old people?

MAKE A CRAZY CHOICE!

Eat fries without salt **OR** doughnuts without sugar?

Be a dove **OR** a hawk?

Put mascara on an eyelash viper **OR** play maracas with a rattlesnake?

The viper might not say thank you: its 'eyelashes' are actually scales to help it camouflage itself

Hide a
llama in your
lunch box...

OR

...a baboon
in your
backpack?

Smack a hippo's bottom...

OR

...tweak a tiger's whiskers?

MAKE A CRAZY CHOICE!

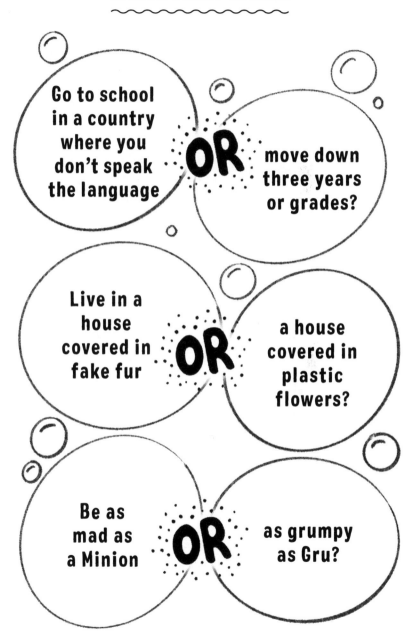

Go to school in a country where you don't speak the language **OR** move down three years or grades?

Live in a house covered in fake fur **OR** a house covered in plastic flowers?

Be as mad as a Minion **OR** as grumpy as Gru?

BRAINY'S TRICKY TRIVIA!

Find a piece of pie on your pillow...

see page 102

OR

...a mysterious love letter?

BRAINY'S TRICKY TRIVIA!

Bounce on a space hopper across the world's smallest desert **snorkel the length of the world's shortest river?**

P103

Find your way to the North Pole using a turtle  **a penguin?**

P106

Paint your bedroom with glow-in-the-dark paint **bright snowshoe yellow paint**

P104

PIE vs LETTER

LET'S START WITH A JOKE.

Q:WHAT IS A MATHEMATICIAN'S FAVOURITE DESSERT?
A:CHERRY PI!

π

This is Pi – or maybe a table with wonky legs

You know, **Pi!** The magic maths number that starts $3.14...$? The one that's used for working out the size of circles? You've never heard of it?! oh **FUGGETTABOUTIT**. That's the last joke I tell you. What do you mean, you're glad?

If you prefer pie to Pi, head to the New York hotel where you get a slice of the tasty one on your pillow: cherry, fudge, pumpkin and other flavours. Yum.

But if you'd like a letter, head to **Italy.** Hotel workers found **OLD LOVE LETTERS** behind a wardrobe, and now you'll get one on your pillow if you stay. How sweet!

Pie `3pts` **Letter** `5pts`

Pie before bedtime? Your dentist would be cross!

HOPPER vs SNORKEL

The **KING OF THE SPACE HOPPER** is Steven Payne. He bounced **76** miles across a mountain range on a child's space hopper (the adult ones were too big to hop up the steep bits). Why? We don't know. Will he do it again? **No.**

Getting across the **WORLD'S SMALLEST DESERT** would be easy. The Carcross Desert in Canada is one square mile. Your biggest problem will be dodging the volleyball players and skydivers who play there.

Still too tough? Grab your snorkel and head to Kuokanjoki, Finland — it's the **WORLD'S SHORTEST RIVER.** Or you could hold your breath instead: it's only **3.5m** long, the length of a (small) car.

Hopper `6pts` Snorkel `2pts`
Bouncing beats a chilly swim!

GLOW vs YELLOW

Do you have **GLOW-IN-THE-DARK** stars, or toys? You shine a light on them, and then they glow? When your grandparents were small, lots more things glowed in the dark like watches with glowing numbers, clocks and compasses. And these glowed without shining a light on them, too — a glow called

Long Word Alert!

radioluminescence.

There was one problem though: the radium paint that made radioluminescence was **HIGHLY POISONOUS**. Even worse, the women who worked in the factories were told it was safe and used to lick the wet end of the paintbrushes they used, to make them pointy. They even painted their nails with it. More than 50 died before the poison paint was banned. There's a new paint now: **YOUR GLOW TOYS ARE TOTALLY SAFE.**

Snowshoe yellow is very bright,

very sunny. And what a funny name! Nobody knows why it's called that. Another name for it is **INDIA YELLOW**. The world-famous artist Van Gogh used it. But, like radium paint, you can't buy it any more.

Why not? Because artists found out how it was made: using COW pee.

"Don't feed me mango leaves," says Daisy

Worse than that, to get the right bright yellow, cows were fed mango leaves. This makes them poorly, but also makes their urine very yellow.

Collect enough of it and you can turn it into the **COLOUR OF SUNFLOWERS** (or, err, snowshoes?!)

Glow (-11 pts) **Yellow** (-11 pts)

One would poison you, the other would poison cows.

TURTLE vs PENGUIN

When you're lost and your dad's phone has run out of battery, what do you do? *TURN ON YOUR PENGUIN,* of course!

Deep inside the earth, metal is sloshing around and causing

"I think it's South. Or North. One of those," says Percy

our planet to emit a magnetic field — that's why we have a North and South Pole, **LIKE A MAGNET.** This protects us from cosmic rays, but it's also used by animals to swim across thousands of miles of oceans, home to breed.

"Dunno. I'm off to the beach," says Terry

Sadly, penguins are strictly South Pole kinda guys while turtles will happily pootle off to most places — but don't like the chilly bits. **YOU'RE ON YOUR OWN.**

Turtle (-3 pts) Penguin (-3 pts)
You should have asked Santa instead.

MAKE A CRAZY CHOICE!

Learn how to swallow swords...

...juggle with fire?

Have a curly tail
like a pig...

OR

...a bushy tail
like a squirrel?

MAKE A CRAZY CHOICE!

Be afraid of door handles **OR** be afraid of rain?

Grow up with wolves **OR** or baboons?

Wake up green like the Hulk **OR** tiny like Ant-Man?

MAKE A CRAZY CHOICE!

Discover a box of war medals in your fishing net  an unexploded bomb?

Dream about your head teacher  dream about the last disgusting meal you ate?

Feel embarrassed  worried?

Get chewing gum in your hair...

...bird poo?

Tip baby food down your underpants...

OR

...wash your hair with it?

MAKE A CRAZY CHOICE!

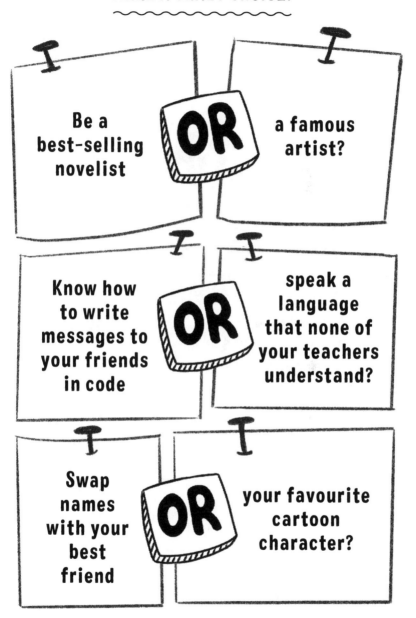

Be a best-selling novelist **OR** a famous artist?

Know how to write messages to your friends in code **OR** speak a language that none of your teachers understand?

Swap names with your best friend **OR** your favourite cartoon character?

Live in Brokenwind **OR** Scratchy Bottom?

P116

Own a pet called Say Little **OR** Potooooooo?

Both have won prizes. Which would you want at home?

P117

Join the gravy train **OR** have your cake and eat it too?

P118

BRAINY'S TRICKY TRIVIA!

Create a tiny model of your favourite person...

OR

...a colossal statue?

see page 119

BROKENWIND vs SCRATCHY BOTTOM

Brokenwind is a hamlet, or tiny village, in Scotland.

Scratchy Bottom is a valley near the Durdle Door beauty spot in England.

The origins of these place names is lost in the mists of time, but I'd like to start by listing the —

"**Hey you!** Hiding at the back of the classroom! No, don't look at your friend, I'm talking to you. Why are you laughing? This isn't funny, you know, this is **HISTORY**. How old do you think you are?

Right, I've had just about enough of your sniggering. Go and see the head teacher **NOW!**"

I've completely forgotten what I was telling you.

Brokenwind 4 pts **Scratchy Bottom** 6 pts

The bottom is top of the class.

SAY LITTLE? OK, you're the boss.

Tumbleweed. You get it in deserts where nothing is happening — or when someone's made a bad joke.

Oh, so you **DO** want to know more? Make your mind up! Say Little was a *greyhound* and won thousands for his owner — who I guess had quite a lot of nice things to say about him.

POTOOOOOOOOO was a racehorse who was supposed to be named Potatoes. The stable boy couldn't spell that, so he wrote Potoooooooo instead. I bet the horse had a lovely jacket* though.

* 100% worst joke in this book. Sorry, no refunds.

Say Little `3pts` **Potoooooooo** `1pt`

A horse named Potatoes wouldn't be any better.

GRAVY vs CAKE

BAD GRAVY NEWS: there's no gravy.

GOOD GRAVY NEWS: this *idiom* means

All aboard the gravy train!

you've got lucky. Someone has given you an easy job for lots of money, or 'gravy' as it was once known. If grandma pays you a pound or a dollar every time you say thank you, then you have a ticket **ON THE GRAVY TRAIN!**

It's bad news all round for cake lovers, though. Once you've had your cake — you've eaten it — it's gone (in your tummy). So you can't *HAVE YOUR CAKE AND EAT IT*, too. If you say someone's trying to do that, they want the impossible.

Cake. Sadly you can only eat it once

They're going to be very **DISAPPOINTED!**

Gravy `3pts` **Cake** `0pts`
Gravy good, cake bad!

TINY vs COLOSSAL

In 2022, a man called **WILLARD WIGAN** made a model of Queen Elizabeth, standing in the 'eye' of the needle. And then he made her a golden

Willard put the Queen in here

carriage, with **200 DIFFERENT PARTS,** and that fits inside a needle, too.

Willard's teachers said he'd never achieve anything because he's autistic — but he calls this his Superpower. Who do you think was right?

If you prefer MASSIVE statues, the **STATUE OF UNITY** in Gujarat, India is as big as 100 men on each others' shoulders, or four Statues of Liberty. It cost a whopping US$420 million (£380m). To get the best view, climb Vallabhbhai Patel and peer out from inside his chest. He won't mind a bit.

Tiny `8pts` **Colossal** `3pts`

David beats Goliath every time!

Have Queen Victoria
as your grandma...

OR

...Abraham Lincoln
as your grandpa?

MAKE A CRAZY CHOICE!

Get a private tour of the White House **OR** Buckingham Palace?

Live without noise **OR** live without silence?

Make your teacher clap whenever you touch your nose **OR** make your parents blow a raspberry when you tug your ear?

MAKE A CRAZY CHOICE!

Make anything you draw come to life  do the same for anything you write about?

Win a staring competition with a stegosaurus  beat a triceratops at the triple jump?

Make sure everyone in the world has enough food  everyone has enough safe drinking water?

MAKE A CRAZY CHOICE!

Wear stinky shoes...

...soggy socks?

Have an ironing board strapped to your back...

...a slinky instead of a knee?

MAKE A CRAZY CHOICE!

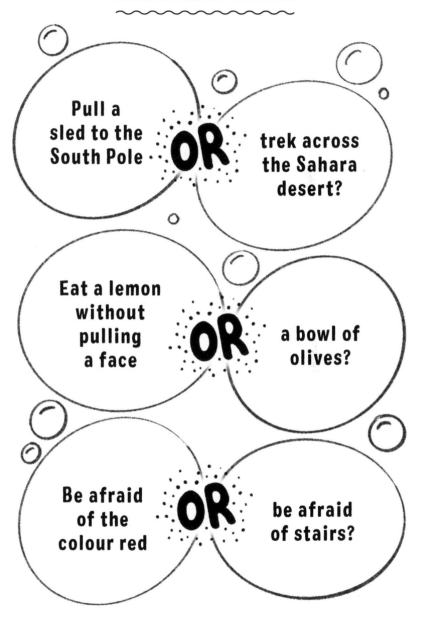

Pull a sled to the South Pole **OR** trek across the Sahara desert?

Eat a lemon without pulling a face **OR** a bowl of olives?

Be afraid of the colour red **OR** be afraid of stairs?

MAKE A CRAZY CHOICE!

Be the world champion Dog Surfer (with your pooch!)...

...the world champion Pumpkin Paddler?

BRAINY'S SCORECARD

Player ❶ .... **Player ❷** ....

Page		Score ❶	Score ❷	Page		Score ❶	Score ❷
10	Shed vs Car			70	Barrel vs Submarine		
12	E vs Vowels			72	Board vs Collar		
13	Astra... vs Somni...			73	Feet vs Ears		
14	Shower vs Elevator			74	Koala vs Baby		
28	Bat vs Dog			84	Adenoid vs Toes		
30	Pennies vs Corn			86	Dog vs Termite		
31	Dribble vs Leftovers			87	Cucumber vs Cabbage		
32	Panda vs Sloth			88	Earwax vs Hair		
42	Elephant vs Chimp			102	Pie vs Letter		
43	Prison vs Hotel			103	Hopper vs Snorkel		
44	Giraffe vs Bird			104	Glow vs Yellow		
46	Ants vs Germs			106	Turtle vs Penguin		
56	Beach vs Highway			116	Broken... vs Scratchy		
57	Salt vs Sugar			117	Say Little vs Potooo...		
58	Logs vs Singing			118	Gravy vs Cake		
59	Coaster vs Cheetos			119	Tiny vs Colossal		
	TOTAL:				GRAND TOTAL:		

One Last Crazy Choice!

I hoped you enjoyed making all these crazy choices. And now you also know more about Scratchy Bottom, dogs in parachutes, sugar and underwater waterfalls. One day, you'll thank me for that.*

Here's your last head scratcher: will you keep this book a secret? Or will you find a way to give your opinion to everyone you know, and millions more you don't? Grown-ups do this all the time – why shouldn't you?

If you have something to say, ask a parent to leave a review wherever they bought this book. (You may need to write it for them – you know what grown-ups are like).

I can't wait to find out what you think!

Mat

*When you go skydiving with your dog in Greenland and land bum-first in a spiky bush, but find a sachet of sugar in your lunch box. It'll happen one day, believe me.

Three More to Try!

Awesome Jokes That Every 8 Year Old Should Know
The best-selling series of jokes that grown-ups love to hear first thing in the morning.

The Cheeky Charlie series
Meet Harriet and her small, stinky brother. Together, they're trouble. Fabulously funny capers for chaos-loving kids!

Fantastic Wordsearches
Wordsearch puzzles with a difference: themed, crossword clues and hidden words await!

Order online or in bookshops, or discover more at
www.matwaugh.co.uk

My Life of Choices

I've made some terrible choices in my life.

✈ When I was six, I dribbled modelling glue on the radiator. I planned to peel it off later (very satisfying). But I forgot, and sat in it instead.

🏚 When I was nine, I dropped an epic water balloon from a bedroom window at my friend's house. It fell inside the house, not outside. It was his parents' bedroom.

🏊 When I was sixteen, I skipped breakfast. In assembly I fainted and fell head-first into a row of children three years below me. I can still hear them laughing.

But then I grew up and I started making excellent decisions!

🐘 I decided that an African elephant wasn't flapping its ears to be friendly, and that we should run. Fast.

🏰 I took a trip to a theme park where I met Mrs Waugh. She wasn't called that then, of course. That would be weird.

➕ I did home improvements in flip-flops. Actually, forget that one: I had to visit hospital with a rusty nail sticking out of my foot. The nurses said that it served me right, and that men of my age shouldn't wear flip-flops.

See? I'm super-wise now, and my family agree (they don't).

What's the best and worst decision *you've* ever made? I'd love to hear from you – your parents can email me!

mail@matwaugh.co.uk

Made in the USA
Middletown, DE
18 December 2023

46115499R00078